the better Mom
PRAYER JOURNAL

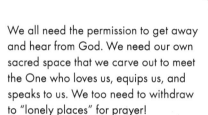

Hi friend!

I need to let you in on something. I want to give you permission; give you a little friendly nudge - *It's ok to get away. And get alone...*

I know that so much of what we do as moms is with others. They're all people we love. We are busy taking care of our home, building our marriage, caring for our children, working, serving at church, and connecting with friends, family, and neighbors. The truth is...most of the time we are not alone!

But did you know it's ok to get away? And get alone? No guilt. Nothing to be ashamed of. Your soul needs it – just like mine.

Of all people, Jesus knew it too. Luke tells us that even as busy, demanding, and purposeful as Jesus' life was, he still *"often withdrew to lonely places and prayed"* (Luke 5:16).

Did you catch that? He *"often"* got away and got alone. His alone time was purposeful though. It wasn't just for the sake of getting some down time or relaxing; Jesus' alone time was to encounter God the Father.

We all need the permission to get away and hear from God. We need our own sacred space that we carve out to meet the One who loves us, equips us, and speaks to us. We too need to withdraw to "lonely places" for prayer!

That's what this prayer journal is all about. In the following pages you'll notice a simple outline on each page for you to write out your prayers, make a list of requests, and keep track of praises. What a privilege and joy it is to bring our prayers to God. Like any good parent, He delights in hearing our hearts.

My prayer is that the following pages would be just that - an opportunity for us, as God's daughters, to pour out our hearts to our Father who loves us, cares for us, and has promised to provide for us. My prayer is that this is a resource that provides an opportunity for you to get away and encounter God's living presence through His Word and through prayer.

Blessings to you my friends, as we run to the throne of grace together!

"Come to me, all you who are weary and burdened, and I will give you rest. Take my yoke upon you and learn from me, for I am gentle and humble in heart, and you will find rest for your souls. For my yoke is easy and my burden is light."

MATTHEW 11:28-30

my praises

....

....

....

....

....

....

my prayers

....

....

....

....

....

....

thoughts	other's prayer requests

my praises

....

....

....

....

....

....

my prayers

....

....

....

....

....

thoughts

_____

_____

_____

_____

other's prayer requests

_____

_____

_____

_____

my praises

my prayers

thoughts

other's prayer requests

my praises

my prayers

thoughts

other's prayer requests

DATE _____ / _____ / _____

my praises

··

··

··

··

··

··

my prayers

··

··

··

··

··

··

thoughts

_____

_____

_____

_____

other's prayer requests

_____

_____

_____

_____

DATE _____ / _____ / _____

my praises

my prayers

thoughts

other's prayer requests

"Do not be anxious about anything, but in every situation, by prayer and petition, with thanksgiving, present your requests to God. And the peace of God, which transcends all understanding, will guard your hearts and your minds in Christ Jesus."

PHILIPPIANS 4:6-7

my praises

my prayers

thoughts

other's prayer requests

DATE _____ / _____ / _____

my praises

my prayers

thoughts

other's prayer requests

my praises

....

....

....

....

....

my prayers

....

....

....

....

....

thoughts

_____

_____

_____

_____

other's prayer requests

_____

_____

_____

_____

my praises

....

....

....

....

....

....

my prayers

....

....

....

....

....

....

thoughts

_____

_____

_____

other's prayer requests

_____

_____

_____

my praises

. . . .

. . . .

. . . .

. . . .

. . . .

. . . .

my prayers

. . . .

. . . .

. . . .

. . . .

. . . .

. . . .

thoughts

other's prayer requests

my praises

my prayers

thoughts

other's prayer requests

PRAY

FATHER, GIVE ME STRENGTH
WHEN I AM WEAK. WHERE I AM
TIRED, GIVE ME GRACE. I NEED
YOUR RESOURCES. FILL ME WITH
YOUR SPIRIT TODAY SO THAT I
CAN BE THE KIND OF MOM YOU
HAVE CALLED ME TO BE. GIVE
ME POWER TO HONOR YOU AND
LOVE MY FAMILY AS I SHOULD.
IN JESUS NAME, AMEN.

my praises

....
....
....
....
....
....

my prayers

....
....
....
....
....
....

thoughts

other's prayer requests

DATE _____ / _____ / _____

my praises

....

....

....

....

....

....

my prayers

....

....

....

....

....

....

thoughts

other's prayer requests

my praises

· ·

· ·

· ·

· ·

· ·

· ·

my prayers

· ·

· ·

· ·

· ·

· ·

thoughts

other's prayer requests

"Do nothing out of
selfish ambition or vain
conceit. Rather, in
humility value others above
yourselves, not looking to
your own interests but
each of you to the interests
of the others."

PHILIPPIANS 2:3-4

my praises

....

....

....

....

....

....

my prayers

....

....

....

....

....

....

thoughts	other's prayer requests

my praises

....

....

....

....

....

....

my prayers

....

....

....

....

....

....

thoughts	other's prayer requests

my praises

. . . .

. . . .

. . . .

. . . .

. . . .

. . . .

my prayers

. . . .

. . . .

. . . .

. . . .

. . . .

thoughts

other's prayer requests

my praises

....

....

....

....

....

....

my prayers

....

....

....

....

....

thoughts

_____

_____

_____

other's prayer requests

_____

_____

_____

DATE _____ / _____ / _____

my praises

my prayers

thoughts

other's prayer requests

DATE _____ / _____ / _____

my praises

my prayers

thoughts

other's prayer requests

"Be joyful in hope,
patient in affliction,
faithful in prayer."

ROMANS 12:12

my praises

....

....

....

....

....

....

my prayers

....

....

....

....

....

....

thoughts

other's prayer requests

DATE _____ / _____ / _____

my praises

....

....

....

....

....

....

my prayers

....

....

....

....

....

thoughts

_____

_____

_____

_____

other's prayer requests

_____

_____

_____

_____

my praises

....

....

....

....

....

....

my prayers

....

....

....

....

....

....

thoughts

other's prayer requests

my praises

....

....

....

....

....

....

my prayers

....

....

....

....

....

....

thoughts	other's prayer requests

DATE _____ / _____ / _____

my praises

. . . .

. . . .

. . . .

. . . .

. . . .

. . . .

my prayers

. . . .

. . . .

. . . .

. . . .

. . . .

. . . .

thoughts	other's prayer requests

my praises

my prayers

thoughts

other's prayer requests

PRAY

FATHER, REPLACE MY FEAR WITH FAITH.
HELP ME NOT TO LOOK AT ALL OF THE
"WHAT-IFS" IN MY LIFE. INSTEAD, GIVE
ME EYES TO LOOK TO YOU. HELP ME TO
REMEMBER YOUR POWER, GOODNESS,
PROMISES, AND TRUTH. I WANT TO
RELEASE ALL OF THE THINGS THAT WEIGH
ME DOWN. I AM GIVING THEM TO YOU
RIGHT NOW, LORD. TAKE THEM. LIGHTEN
MY LOAD. I AM PLACING THEM IN YOUR
HANDS BECAUSE THEY ARE TOO HEAVY
FOR ME TO CARRY. I TRUST YOU. TODAY, I
AM GOING TO WALK IN FAITH INSTEAD OF
BEING GRIPPED BY FEAR.
IN JESUS NAME, AMEN.

my praises

....

....

....

....

....

....

my prayers

....

....

....

....

....

....

thoughts

other's prayer requests

DATE _____ / _____ / _____

my praises

....

....

....

....

....

....

my prayers

....

....

....

....

....

....

thoughts

....

....

....

....

other's prayer requests

....

....

....

....

my praises

....
....
....
....
....
....

my prayers

....
....
....
....
....

thoughts

_____
_____
_____

other's prayer requests

_____
_____
_____

"The Lord is my rock,
my fortress and my deliverer;
my God is my rock, in whom I
take refuge, my shield and the
horn of my salvation,
my stronghold."

PSALM 18:2

my praises

....

....

....

....

....

....

my prayers

....

....

....

....

....

....

thoughts

_____

_____

_____

_____

other's prayer requests

_____

_____

_____

_____

DATE _____ / _____ / _____

my praises

....

....

....

....

....

....

my prayers

....

....

....

....

....

thoughts

other's prayer requests

my praises

my prayers

thoughts

other's prayer requests

my praises

....

....

....

....

....

....

my prayers

....

....

....

....

....

....

thoughts

other's prayer requests

my praises

. . . .

. . . .

. . . .

. . . .

. . . .

. . . .

my prayers

. . . .

. . . .

. . . .

. . . .

. . . .

. . . .

thoughts

other's prayer requests

my praises

....

....

....

....

....

....

my prayers

....

....

....

....

....

....

thoughts	other's prayer requests

"Trust in the Lord with all your heart and lean not on your own understanding; in all your ways submit to him, and he will make your paths straight."

PROVERBS 3:5-6

my praises

. . . .

. . . .

. . . .

. . . .

. . . .

. . . .

my prayers

. . . .

. . . .

. . . .

. . . .

. . . .

thoughts	other's prayer requests

DATE _____ / _____ / _____

my praises

. . . .

. . . .

. . . .

. . . .

. . . .

. . . .

my prayers

. . . .

. . . .

. . . .

. . . .

. . . .

thoughts

other's prayer requests

my praises

. . . .

. . . .

. . . .

. . . .

. . . .

. . . .

my prayers

. . . .

. . . .

. . . .

. . . .

. . . .

thoughts

other's prayer requests

my praises

....

....

....

....

....

my prayers

....

....

....

....

....

thoughts	other's prayer requests

DATE _____ / _____ / _____

my praises

· ·

· ·

· ·

· ·

· ·

· ·

my prayers

· ·

· ·

· ·

· ·

· ·

thoughts

other's prayer requests

my praises

. . . .

. . . .

. . . .

. . . .

. . . .

. . . .

my prayers

. . . .

. . . .

. . . .

. . . .

. . . .

thoughts

other's prayer requests

"Only be careful, and watch yourselves closely so that you do not forget the things your eyes have seen or let them fade from your heart as long as you live. Teach them to your children and to their children after them."

DEUTERONOMY 4:9

my praises

my prayers

thoughts

other's prayer requests

my praises

my prayers

thoughts

other's prayer requests

my praises

....

....

....

....

....

....

my prayers

....

....

....

....

....

thoughts	other's prayer requests

DATE _____ / _____ / _____

my praises

my prayers

thoughts

other's prayer requests

my praises

....

....

....

....

....

....

my prayers

....

....

....

....

....

....

thoughts

_____

_____

_____

_____

other's prayer requests

_____

_____

_____

_____

my praises

....

....

....

....

....

....

my prayers

....

....

....

....

....

....

thoughts

_____

_____

_____

_____

other's prayer requests

_____

_____

_____

_____

PRAY

FATHER, YOUR WORD SAYS
YOU ARE A ROCK. YOU ARE A
HIDING PLACE – A REFUGE.
BE MY ROCK TODAY. WOULD
YOU BE MY HIDING PLACE? BE
MY REFUGE – THE SAFE PLACE
FOR MY SOUL TO BE STILL. I
LOVE YOU LORD, MY STRENGTH
COMES FROM YOU. TEACH ME
TO RUN TO YOU AND FIND MY
TRUE SAFETY, STRENGTH, AND
SECURITY IN YOU ALONE. IN
JESUS NAME, AMEN.

my praises

my prayers

thoughts

other's prayer requests

DATE _____ / _____ / _____

my praises

· ·

· ·

· ·

· ·

· ·

· ·

my prayers

· ·

· ·

· ·

· ·

· ·

thoughts

_____

_____

_____

_____

other's prayer requests

_____

_____

_____

_____

my praises

my prayers

thoughts

other's prayer requests

"Peace I leave with you; my peace I give you. I do not give to you as the world gives. Do not let your hearts be troubled and do not be afraid."

JOHN 14:27

my praises

....

....

....

....

....

....

my prayers

....

....

....

....

....

....

thoughts	other's prayer requests

my praises

my prayers

thoughts

other's prayer requests

my praises

my prayers

thoughts

other's prayer requests

my praises

....

....

....

....

....

....

my prayers

....

....

....

....

....

....

thoughts

_____

_____

_____

_____

other's prayer requests

_____

_____

_____

_____

DATE _____ / _____ / _____

my praises

. . . .

. . . .

. . . .

. . . .

. . . .

. . . .

my prayers

. . . .

. . . .

. . . .

. . . .

. . . .

thoughts

other's prayer requests

my praises

....

....

....

....

....

....

my prayers

....

....

....

....

....

....

thoughts

_____

_____

_____

_____

other's prayer requests

_____

_____

_____

_____

"Praise be to the God and Father of our Lord Jesus Christ! In his great mercy he has given us new birth into a living hope through the resurrection of Jesus Christ from the dead, and into an inheritance that can never perish, spoil or fade. This inheritance is kept in heaven for you, who through faith are shielded by God's power until the coming of the salvation that is ready to be revealed in the last time."

1 PETER 1:3-5

DATE _____ / _____ / _____

my praises

my prayers

thoughts

other's prayer requests

DATE _____ / _____ / _____

my praises

my prayers

thoughts

other's prayer requests

my praises

....

....

....

....

....

....

my prayers

....

....

....

....

....

thoughts

other's prayer requests

my praises

....

....

....

....

....

....

my prayers

....

....

....

....

....

....

thoughts

_____

_____

_____

_____

other's prayer requests

_____

_____

_____

_____

my praises

....

....

....

....

....

....

my prayers

....

....

....

....

....

....

thoughts	other's prayer requests

my praises

....

....

....

....

....

....

my prayers

....

....

....

....

....

thoughts	other's prayer requests

PRAY

FATHER, GREAT IS YOUR
FAITHFULNESS. YOU ARE STEADY.
I CAN ALWAYS COUNT ON YOU. YOU
ALWAYS DO WHAT YOU SAY. YOU
NEVER GROW WEARY OR LEAVE ME
ALONE. YOU HAVE PROMISED TO
NEVER FORSAKE ME. THANK YOU
FOR YOUR ENDURING LOVE AND
FOR ALWAYS BEING THERE – BEING
HERE FOR ME. I DON'T ALWAYS
KNOW YOUR PLANS, BUT I WILL
TRUST YOUR PLANS. I WILL TRUST
YOU BECAUSE I KNOW YOU ARE
FAITHFUL AND GOOD.
IN JESUS NAME, AMEN.

my praises

....

....

....

....

....

....

my prayers

....

....

....

....

....

....

thoughts

_____

_____

_____

_____

other's prayer requests

_____

_____

_____

_____

my praises

. . . .

. . . .

. . . .

. . . .

. . . .

. . . .

my prayers

. . . .

. . . .

. . . .

. . . .

. . . .

. . . .

thoughts	other's prayer requests

DATE _____ / _____ / _____

my praises

. . . .

. . . .

. . . .

. . . .

. . . .

. . . .

my prayers

. . . .

. . . .

. . . .

. . . .

. . . .

thoughts

other's prayer requests

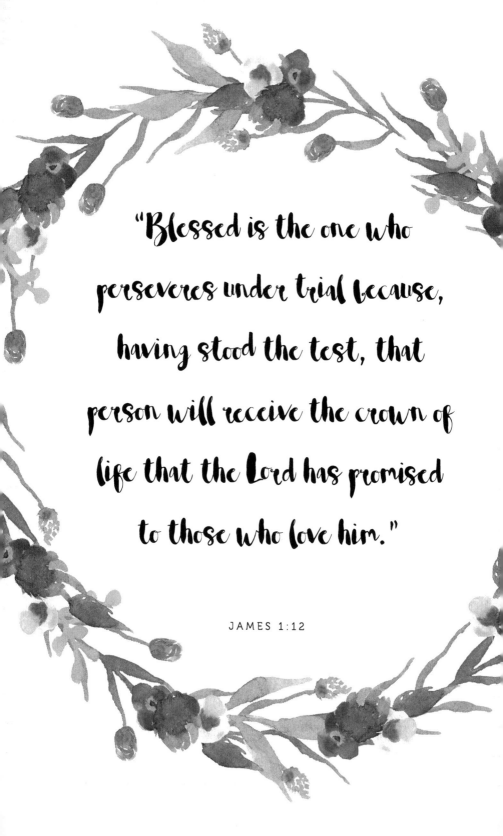

"Blessed is the one who perseveres under trial because, having stood the test, that person will receive the crown of life that the Lord has promised to those who love him."

JAMES 1:12

DATE _____ / _____ / _____

my praises

....
....
....
....
....
....

my prayers

....
....
....
....
....

thoughts

_____
_____
_____
_____

other's prayer requests

_____
_____
_____
_____

DATE _____ / _____ / _____

my praises

· ·

· ·

· ·

· ·

· ·

· ·

my prayers

· ·

· ·

· ·

· ·

· ·

thoughts

other's prayer requests

my praises

my prayers

thoughts

other's prayer requests

my praises

. . . .

. . . .

. . . .

. . . .

. . . .

. . . .

my prayers

. . . .

. . . .

. . . .

. . . .

. . . .

thoughts

other's prayer requests

DATE _____ / _____ / _____

my praises

....

....

....

....

....

....

my prayers

....

....

....

....

....

....

thoughts

_____

_____

_____

_____

other's prayer requests

_____

_____

_____

_____

my praises

....

....

....

....

....

....

my prayers

....

....

....

....

....

thoughts

_____

_____

_____

_____

other's prayer requests

_____

_____

_____

_____

PRAY

FATHER, I CONFESS MY SINS TO YOU.
I ADMIT THAT I FALL SHORT OF WHO
YOU CALL ME TO BE. I KNOW THAT I
CAN BE SELFISH AND PRIDEFUL. THANK
YOU THAT JESUS HAS BEEN OBEDIENT
WHERE I HAVE BEEN DISOBEDIENT. HE
HAS BEEN FAITHFUL WHERE I HAVE BEEN
UNFAITHFUL. JESUS ALONE HAS BEEN
HOLY WHERE I HAVE BEEN UNHOLY.
CREATE IN ME A NEW HEART – A HEART
LIKE CHRIST'S. HELP ME TO SAY NO TO
MY SINFUL NATURE AND INSTEAD BE
ALIVE TO CHRIST WHO LIVES IN ME. GIVE
ME GRACE TODAY AS I TURN FROM MY SIN
AND TRUST IN MY SAVIOR.
IN JESUS NAME, AMEN.

my praises

....

....

....

....

....

....

my prayers

....

....

....

....

....

....

thoughts

_____

_____

_____

_____

other's prayer requests

_____

_____

_____

_____

DATE ____ / ____ / ____

my praises

my prayers

thoughts

other's prayer requests

my praises

....

....

....

....

....

....

my prayers

....

....

....

....

....

....

thoughts	other's prayer requests

my praises

....

....

....

....

....

....

my prayers

....

....

....

....

....

....

....

thoughts

_____

_____

_____

other's prayer requests

_____

_____

_____

my praises

. . . .

. . . .

. . . .

. . . .

. . . .

. . . .

my prayers

. . . .

. . . .

. . . .

. . . .

. . . .

. . . .

thoughts

other's prayer requests

my praises

my prayers

thoughts

other's prayer requests

"Weeping may stay for the night, but rejoicing comes in the morning."

PSALM 30:5

DATE _____ / _____ / _____

my praises

my prayers

thoughts

other's prayer requests

DATE ____ / ____ / ____

my praises

....

....

....

....

....

....

my prayers

....

....

....

....

....

....

thoughts

_____

_____

_____

_____

other's prayer requests

_____

_____

_____

_____

my praises

....

....

....

....

....

....

my prayers

....

....

....

....

....

thoughts	other's prayer requests

my praises

my prayers

thoughts

other's prayer requests

DATE _____ / _____ / _____

my praises

· ·

· ·

· ·

· ·

· ·

· ·

my prayers

· ·

· ·

· ·

· ·

· ·

· ·

thoughts

_____

_____

_____

_____

other's prayer requests

_____

_____

_____

_____

DATE _____ / _____ / _____

my praises

....
....
....
....
....
....

my prayers

....
....
....
....
....

thoughts

_____
_____
_____
_____

other's prayer requests

_____
_____
_____
_____

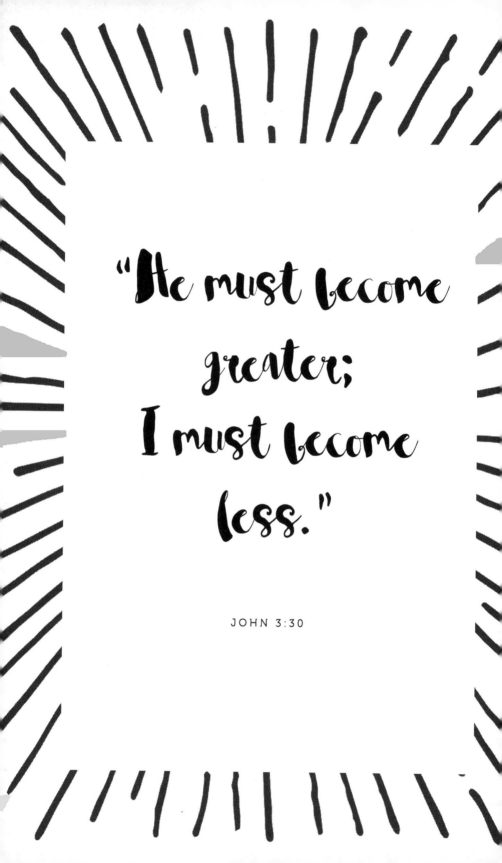

"He must become
greater;
I must become
less."

JOHN 3:30

my praises

....

....

....

....

....

....

my prayers

....

....

....

....

....

thoughts

_____

_____

_____

_____

other's prayer requests

_____

_____

_____

_____

DATE ____ / ____ / ____

my praises

....

....

....

....

....

....

my prayers

....

....

....

....

....

thoughts	other's prayer requests

my praises

....

....

....

....

....

....

my prayers

....

....

....

....

....

thoughts

other's prayer requests

my praises

....

....

....

....

....

....

my prayers

....

....

....

....

....

thoughts

_____

_____

_____

_____

other's prayer requests

_____

_____

_____

_____

my praises

···

···

···

···

···

···

my prayers

···

···

···

···

···

thoughts

_____

_____

_____

_____

other's prayer requests

_____

_____

_____

_____

DATE _____ / _____ / _____

my praises

....
....
....
....
....
....

my prayers

....
....
....
....
....
....

thoughts

other's prayer requests

It is just incredible that you have taken the time over these last few months to spend time with God in prayer and I would love nothing more than to be an encouragement to you in the future.

If you are looking for a community
to connect with other moms

the better Mom.com

is the place for you!

At The Better Mom our mission is to build God-honoring homes by inspiring moms to be better moms through sharing life and learning together.

We believe God has placed a high calling on our lives as we : raise children to impact the world, take care of our homes, love our husbands, and ultimately honor God with our lives.

We would love to have you join our community and share in our journey!

Join in with us!

Made in the USA
San Bernardino, CA
23 October 2018